Dental Marketing

20 Things Every Dentist Should Know About Dental Marketing

Claude W. Bailey III
1st Edition

Dental Marketing

By

Claude W. Bailey III

PUBLISHED BY:

Weston Bailey LLC

Copyright 2014 Weston Bailey, LLC

Special Offer / Register This Book

Dental marketing strategies are constantly changing over time. Register this book to ensure you are kept up to date with the latest strategies. In addition, you will receive the following items, that couldn't, for obvious reasons, be included in the book:

- Free Mobile Website with 30 day trial of capture, connect and close marketing tool
- Google+ for Business Page Guide and Video Tutorial
- Google AdWords offer code
- A few more bonuses that will pleasurably surprise you.

To get your bonuses, send a copy of your receipt to **Bonuses@TheDentalMarketingBook.com** and you'll receive the first bonus immediately.

About The Author

Claude W. Bailey III is an entrepreneur, engineer, author and coach. He is the CEO and Founder of Weston Bailey, LLC a digital marketing agency that helps entrepreneurs capture, connect and close new customers. He strongly believes in leveraging technology to automate the marketing process so the entrepreneur can have the lifestyle he believes he should have for owning a successful business. In Claude's spare time he enjoys educating children through coaching youth basketball, teaching Children's Church, and serving on the school board.

From The Author

I published this book to help dentist achieve the lifestyle they are seeking. The recession of 2008 was an eye opener for many American families and businesses. With the lost of jobs, families lost their health and dental insurance, which kept them from the dentist. Some dentist offices were able to weather the storm, by cutting office hours from 40 hours to 24 hours per week. Others were not so fortunate. Now in 2014 the economy is showing signs of a strong recovery. People are getting employed with benefits again, so how will dentist take advantage of this new growth. I strongly believe digital marketing is the future of dental marketing. I want to help as many dentists consistently capture, connect and close enough new families to achieve the monthly gross revenue they desire to live the lifestyle of their dreams.

Table of Contents

What is Dental Marketing ...7

Top Reason Practices Fail...9

    Top reason for success...10

Marketing A Dental Practice...10

Dental Marketing Ideas...10

How To Capture New Dental Patients...12

How to Get People to Find You...12

Dental Marketing Plan Essentials...13

Required Number of New Dental Patients to Generate Desired Revenue...17

Dental Marketing Return on Investment...19

What To Look For In A Dental Marketing Company...20

Direct Mail Marketing...20

Effectiveness of Direct Mail...21

Internet Marketing...21

Mobile Friendly Website…22

Mobile Website ROI…23

Text Message Marketing…24

3 Benefits of Google AdWords…25

Top Ten Requirements for a Search Engine Optimize (SEO) Website…26

Landing Page versus Main Website…28

Digital Dental Marketing Cost…30

What is Dental Marketing?

Dental marketing is the process of creating consumer interest in your specific dental service. It is a series of action steps taken to get new and current customers to know you, like you and trust you. Once a person trusts you they are more likely to pay you to take care of their dental needs.

Most marketers use a general formula to guide them in the process of a marketing campaign called A.I.D.A.S, which is an acronym for Awareness, Interest, Desire, Action, and Satisfaction. The theory is simply, making people <u>aware</u> of your service in a way that creates <u>interest</u> in learning more about your service to the point of a strong <u>desire</u> to use your service to solve their problem, thereby triggering a buy <u>action</u> with the hope to be completely <u>satisfied</u>.

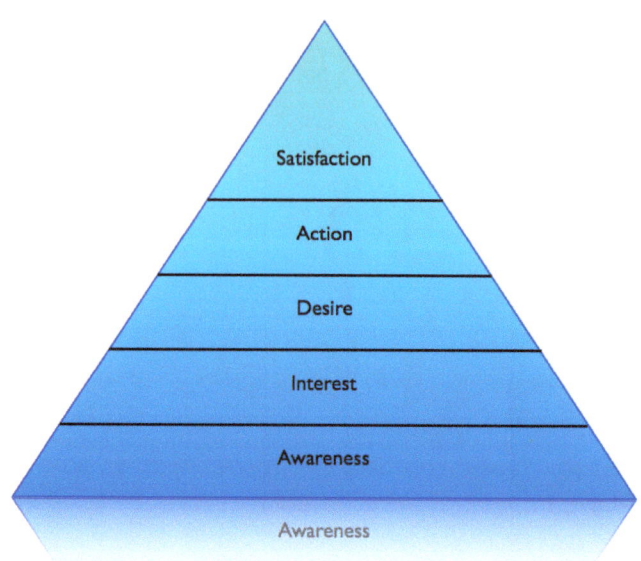

A.I.D.A.S Marketing Formula

Top Reason Practices Fail

Weak sales are a top reason why businesses fail and it applies to dental practices as well. Weak sales are a direct result of failing to overcome five hurtful challenges of owning a business.

1. The lack of competitive edge in a crowded market
2. The lack of a clear marketing funnel
3. The lack of a plan
4. The lack of finding new customers

5. The lack of retaining customers.

Standing out in a crowded market of dentists is one of the most challenging aspects of operating a dental practice. A quick look in the Yellow Pages shows there is a significant amount of competition. 40% of business owners don't think that their business has a competitive advantage reported by the Panel Study of Entrepreneurial Dynamics.

For small or start-up dental practices offering lower prices can put your business in negative cash flow, leading to bad credit, then ultimately out of business. It's also hard to state superior quality because everyone states that and in fact people expect it. However, there are two methods that successful businesses use to positively standout. They are creative ideas to address customer needs and the due diligence of following up. Unfortunately, as many as 48% of marketing campaigns never follow up with a prospect or customer. Failure to follow with prospects and customers is one of the biggest mistakes that businesses make resulting in countless missed opportunities.

TOP REASON FOR SUCCESS

Prospect conversions speak volumes about the success of a business. Only 2% of sales are made on the first contact, 3% on the second, 5% on the third, 10% on the fourth, and an amazing 80% on the fifth to twelfth contact.

Marketing A Dental Practice

Dental marketing should position the dentist as the leading dental professional expert in your service area. The marketing content should inform potential customers with valuable information rather than just buy form me. Give them information that answers their questions or answers questions they should ask. Then spread these question and answers everywhere online and in direct mail.

Dental Marketing Ideas

Develop a clear marketing funnel that will make people aware, interested, desire, take action and become completely satisfied. Here is a high level strategy.

Use micro-blog sites to promote all content created to capture the attention and lead people to a landing page that creates interest and a desire for them to give you their contact information to learn more about your dental services. You then deliver more information about your service leading them eventually to select you as their dentist.

Online Marketing Plan

How To Capture New Dental Patients

There are a lot of good ways to find new dental patients, such as direct mail, Internet advertising, and even video and radio commercials to name a few. However, all or one alone will only get your limited exposure unless it is a part of a complete marketing funnel. I recommend developing a complete marketing funnel that first positions you as an expert that is everywhere showing prospects how your can solve their problem. Then show them satisfied customers that use your service to solve their dental needs.

How to Get People to Find You

One of the quickest ways to attract prospects that are looking for a dentist office is to be present on the Internet. 88% of smart phone owners use their cell phone to search for local businesses and take action within the same day according to research reported by Google, Inc. Here is how to take advantage of this fact.

First claim your Google+ local page, it is free presently at the writing of this book! Visit Google+ Page web address, plus.google.com. Then click on the link Google+ for business for more information and to get started. The only requirement is to have a physical business address and phone number. A website is not required. Once you claim your business page, promote it with Google's Pay Per Click service Google AdWords Express.

When you register this book by sending a copy of your receipt to this email address, bonus@thedentalmarketingbook.com, you will receive the latest documents and videos on how to set up your Google+ for business page. One of the videos will show you how I created a Google+ for business page for a client.

Dental Marketing Plan Essentials

What should be included in a dental marketing plan? There are three important sections of a marketing plan. First is a description of your target market. Every plan should have a complete market analysis, which includes demographics, psychographics, market trends, and keyword research.

The second important factor to describe is the marketing funnel strategy. How will you make people aware of your service that will lead them to eventually select you as their dentist?

The last important section is customer service. Explain how you will serve your customers to make their life easier and empowering.

Here is a complete marketing plan outline for review.

Marketing Plan Outline

I. Overview and Goals of Marketing Strategy

    A. Marketing Strategy Overview

        1. Who are your customers and competitors?

        2. What problems will your business solve? What are you selling and what price?

        3. Where is your target market located and where can you reach them?

        4. When are your customers most likely to buy?

        5. How will you reach your customers?

B. Marketing Strategy Goals

    1. What is the goal of your marketing campaign? Is it to create a strong brand, build a strong customer base and or increase sales?

II. Target Market Analysis

  A. Target Market

    1. Demographics - statistical data of a population

    2. Psychographics - lifestyle of a particular demographic

    3. Niche market - specialized market area

  B. Competition

    1. Description of major competitors

    2. Assessment of strengths and weaknesses

  C. Market Trends

    1. Industry Trends

    2. Target Market Trends

  D. Market Research

    1. Methods of Research

III. Marketing Strategy

  A. General Description

    1. Marketing effort allocation - percentage of budget allocated to the various marketing strategies online and offline

    2. Discussion on the strategies that are expected to generate the most new business

  B. Sales and Distribution Method

1. Where will you sale and distribute your product and service to the customer... Stores, Offices, Kiosks, Catalogs, Direct Mail, Website, etc.

C. Packaging - If selling a product how will it be packaged.

D. Pricing

1. Price Strategy

a) How low can you charge and make a profit? How high will the market bear? What will you charge and why?

2. Competitive Position

a) Is your price going to be less than, equal to, or greater than your competitors? Why?

E. Branding

1. What is your image?

F. Marketing Database

1. How do you plan to collect and study buying patterns of your customer for future services and products?

G. Sales Strategies

1. How will you contact, deliver and follow-up with sales material to your target market?

a) Direct Sales

b) Direct Mail

c) Email Marketing

d) Affiliate Marketing

e) Reciprocal Marketing

f) Viral Marketing

   g) Digital Marketing

 H. Sales Incentives and Promotions

  1. What incentives or promotions will you use to capture prospects

   a) Free Samples

   b) Cash Back

   c) Sweepstakes, Contest

   d) Online Promotions

   e) Bonuses

   f) Rebates

 I. Advertising Strategies

  1. Traditional Advertising (television, radio, print)

  2. Digital Advertising (banner ads, pay per click, smart phones, portals, interactive TV)

  3. Long-term Sponsorships

 J. Public Relations

  1. How will you build credibility in the marketplace? How will you build an online presence through community groups, clubs, chats, and message boards?

  2. Will you have an event to attract people to your business?

  3. Will you have press releases?

  4. Will you conduct interviews?

 K. Networking

IV. Customer Service

    A. Customer Service Activities

    B. Expected Outcome

V. Marketing Strategy Implementation

    A. In-house responsibility

    B. Outsourced Functions

        1. Advertising, public relations, marketing firms

        2. Advertising networks

        3. Other

VI. Marketing Assessment

    A. In the beginning this section will be blank. After three months evaluate your marketing results compared to your plan. Describe in this section what is working and what is failing. Remember a business and marketing plan is a living document. Meaning it should grow and improve with your business.

Required Number of New Dental Patients to Generate Desired Revenue

Here is the four-step process to calculating the number of monthly new dental patients (MNDP) required each month to generate your desired gross monthly revenue.

1. Determine desired monthly gross revenue (DMGR) by taking overhead monthly expenses and adding your desired gross monthly profit.

2. Determine percentage of gross revenue from new dental patients (%GRNDP). A good rule of thumb, 100% for new practices and 25% for established practices.

3. Determine the average monthly revenue per new patient (AMRNP). Use price for a general cleaning if you don't now where to start.

4. Calculate total number of required monthly new dental patients to achieve desired monthly gross revenue.

$$MNDP = (DMGR)(\%GRNDP) / AMRNP$$

As an example lets say Dr. Sam wants to calculate the number of monthly new dental patients required to maintain desired monthly revenue. Dr. Sam has been in practice for three years and is establishing a good patient base of loyal customers. The overhead expenses add up to $33,300 per month. The desired monthly profit for a rainy day fund and expansion is $26,700. Therefore the total desired monthly gross revenue is $60,000. Over the past year Dr. Sam's average monthly revenue is $37,650, just making the expenses. Now that Dr. Sam revenue is enough to cover the expenses, the desired new gross revenue should come from 40% of new patients. Based on Dr. Sam's prices the average monthly revenue per new dental patient is $300. Therefore, Dr. Sam's monthly new dental patient requirement to achieve monthly gross revenue of $60,000 is:

$$MNDP = (\$60{,}000)(0.40) / \$300 = 80$$

Dr. Sam must see 80 new dental patients a month to generate the $60,000 monthly gross revenue.

Dental Marketing Return on Investment

What is a good dental marketing return on investment? A return of investment (ROI) greater than or equal to three (three hundred percent) is a good general target. In simple terms for every dollar invested in marketing expect at least three dollars in return revenue. Here is the formula to calculate return on investment.

ROI = (Revenue - Marketing Investment) / Marketing Investment

As an example when Dr. Sam invests $2,000 a month in advertising and marketing, he should receive $8,000 in revenue. Then the return on investment is 3 or 300%.

$$ROI = (\$8,000 - \$2,000) / \$2,000 = 3$$

So how would you calculate the appropriate amount of money to invest in marketing to achieve your desired monthly revenue? Let's use the example of Dr. Sam again. Dr. Sam has a desire to gross $60,000 a month in revenue. Of that gross revenue the expectation is that 40% of it comes from new dental patients, which is $24,000. The amount Dr. Sam can expect to invest in marketing to gain new prospects is calculated by re-arranging the ROI equation.

$$\text{Marketing Investment} = \text{Revenue} / (ROI + 1)$$

Therefore expecting a 300% dental marketing return on investment, Dr. Sam should expect to invest $6,000.

$$\text{Marketing Investment} = \$24,000 / (3 + 1) = \$6,000$$

What To Look For In A Dental Marketing Company

What should a dentist look for in a dental marketing company? Simply, look for a company that can deliver a positive marketing return on investment. Marketing is an investment with the goal to make you more money. The general rule of thumb is a 300% return on investment is a good percentage.

Direct Mail Marketing

What is direct mail marketing? Direct mail marketing is the process of physically sending information through the mail to potential prospects to generate consumer awareness, interest, desire, action and satisfaction.

Effectiveness of Direct Mail

Is direct mail marketing effective? Often people label direct mail as junk mail. However, like anything in life, poor planning will lead to poor results. Direct mail marketing is effective if planned and executed correctly. To maximize the return, it is recommended you combine direct mail marketing with digital dental marketing. The marketing return on investment could reach as high as 300%.

Internet Marketing

What is Internet marketing also called digital marketing? It is the process of creating consumer interest in a product or service using the Internet. It is a series of action steps conducted over the Internet to grow new and current consumer interest in a product or service to the point of where they have to have it. The proven marketing formula, A.I.D.A.S (Awareness, Interest, Desire, Action, Satisfaction), still applies.

Mobile Friendly Website

As a primary local dentist do you need a mobile-friendly website? Yes, mobile is very important for local dentist offices. With fierce competition a mobile-friendly website will set you apart among consumers and search engines. 95% of smart phone users look for local information on their phones when at home or out and about according Google, Inc's published report the Google Initiative Agency Guide.

Ten Mobile Best Practices

1. Easy To Scan
2. Simple Navigation
3. Thumb Friendly
4. Easy To Read
5. Mobile Device Compatibility
6. Focus On Conversion
7. Local Presence
8. Seamless
9. Mobile Redirects
10. User Centric

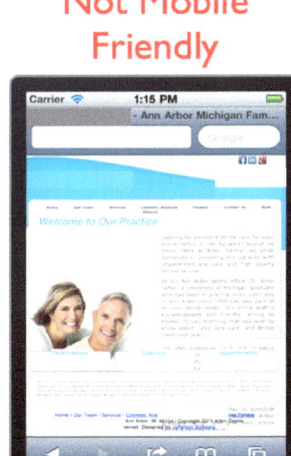 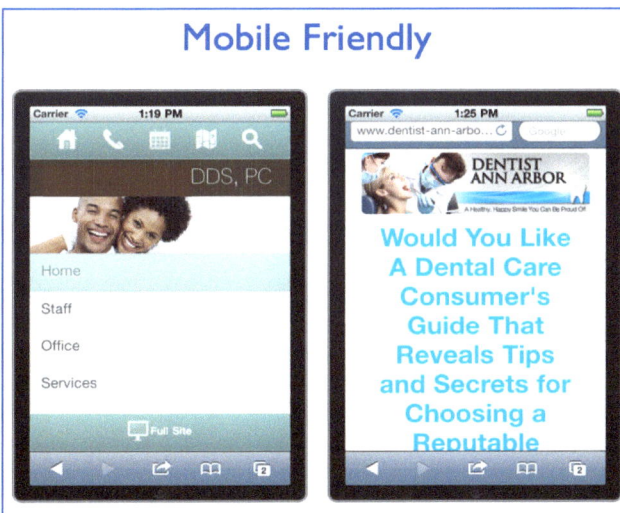

Which one do you like?

Mobile Website ROI

How do you know if a mobile website will help your dental practice gain new dental patients? By measuring and tracking traffic to your website. Use Webmaster analytical tools, such as Google Analytics to track and measure traffic. Also using pay per click advertising through Google AdWords, you can create, track and measure mobile specific campaigns. One of the benefits of the combined use of Google Analytics and AdWords is the ability to calculate actual return on investment.

Text Message Marketing

Why would my dental practice need a text message marketing campaign? There are a lot of reasons, but let's look at statistics to prove the importance of text messaging.

According to Pew Internet as of May 2013 91% of American adults have a cell phone. 67% of cell phone owners check their phone for messages, alerts, or calls even when they don't notice their phone ringing or vibrating. 44% have the phone close to their bed in case of a call or text message. 29% cannot imagine living with out their cell phone. Lastly, 80% of cell phone owners use their cell phone to send or receive text messages. Oh, by the way 31% search for health or medical information online. The statistics go on.

To see how simple it is to use text messaging to deliver information quickly to a prospect, send a text message to 586-522-4055 with your first name and email address. In return you receive instructions from me on how to setup your free custom mobile website.

3 Benefits of Google AdWords

Google AdWords is paid online advertising known as pay per click advertising. The benefits for dental marketing are the following:

1. Relevance: precisely target ads to users based on their interest, location, language, and demographics

2. Return on Investment (ROI): completely measurable allowing accurate calculation of return on investment

3. Reach: capture any segment of the millions of searches worldwide seeking for solutions and answers to their problem.

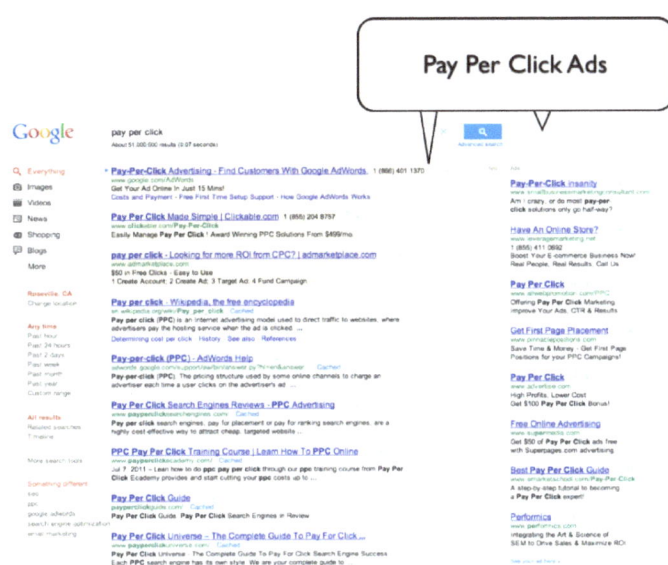

Location of Pay Per Click Ads on Google Search Results

Top Ten Requirements for a Search Engine Optimize (SEO) Website

Here are the top ten items a website must have in order for search engines need, such as Google, to find your website and categorize it by topic. This information comes directly from Google, Inc's "Google Search Engine Optimization Starter Guide".

1. Unique and accurate page titles.
2. Use the description meta tag for each page.
3. Easy to navigate site structure and urls.
4. Quality content.
5. Use keyword anchor text.
6. Optimize use of images.
7. Use header tags appropriately.

8. Notify search engine of your desktop and mobile sites.
9. Promote website with back links.
10. Use webmaster tools.

For complete details read the Google Search Engine Optimization Starter Guide. When you register this book we will send you the current link to download the guide.

Landing Page versus Main Website

Do you need a landing page (mini-website) for your dental practice even if you already have a website? Yes, when you want to be at the top of search engines. Landing pages or mini-websites help implement SEO tip #9, promote website with back links.

Based on a study conduct by HubSpot and published in their report, Lead Generation Lessons From 4,000 Businesses, business with 31 to 40 landing pages received seven times more leads than businesses with only one to five landing pages. Businesses that service consumers directly with over 40 landing pages receive ten times more leads than business with only one to five landing pages.

Why so many landing pages? Each landing page should focus on one topic and one action. For example a general family dental practice can have a lot of specific services besides general cleaning. A practice can perform root canals, crowns and bridging, teeth whitening, implants, and pediatric dentistry to name a few. So a dental practice would have a specific landing page (mini-website) for each of these services asking the reader to take a specific action to

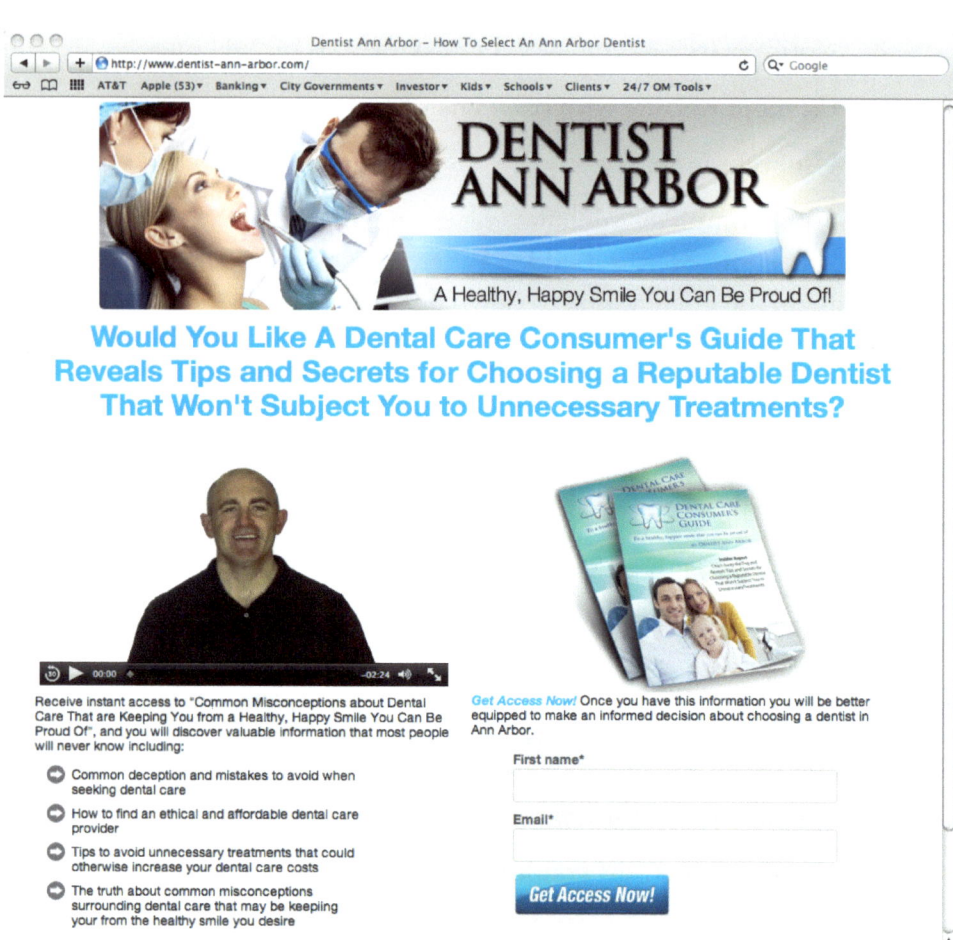

receive more information on the topic. In addition, each landing page would include a link back to your main website.

Landing Page Example

Digital Dental Marketing Cost

The cost of digital dental marketing varies depending on the service. For example some companies offer local search engine optimization for only $225 per month, with an initial setup fee of $1,750. For the same service another company requires an initial setup investment of $3,500 and $500 per month. In general a complete Internet marketing campaign can start as low as $3000 per month. The age-old proverb "you get what you pay for" applies with digital (Internet) marketing services.

Remember to look for a company that will provide you a 300% return on your marketing investment. Higher desired revenue will in general require a higher upfront investment. Go through the exercise again to determine the required marketing investment to achieve your desired monthly gross revenue.

Now What?

You deserve to be found by patients you desire to serve. As mentioned in the beginning of the book, I want to keep in communication with you. When you send your receipt to Bonuses@TheDentalMarketingBook.com, not only will you receive the bonus package listed, but also there are a few other things coming your way that will help tremendously.

Sources Cited

1. Small Biz Trends, http://smallbiztrends.com/2011/09/why-do-most-start-ups-fail.html

2. Follow Up Success, http://www.followupsuccess.com/2011/02/21/shocking-sales-statistics-as-it-relates-to-follow-up/

3. Google, Inc, A Google Initiative Agency Guide, http://howtogomo.com

www.ingramcontent.com/pod-product-compliance
Lightning Source LLC
Chambersburg PA
CBHW040820200526

45159CB00024B/3060